LEAVING AND LEAVING YOU

Also by Sophie Hannah from Carcanet

The Hero and the Girl Next Door
Hotels like Houses

SOPHIE HANNAH

LEAVING AND LEAVING YOU

CARCANET

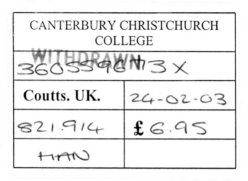
First published in 1999 by
Carcanet Press Limited
4th Floor, Conavon Court
12-16 Blackfriars Street
Manchester M3 5BQ

A CIP catalogue record for this book
is available from the British Library
ISBN 1 85754 407 2

The publisher acknowledges financial assistance
from the Arts Council of England

Funded by
THE
ARTS
COUNCIL
OF ENGLAND

Set in 10pt Palatino by Bryan Williamson, Frome
Printed and bound in England by SRP Ltd, Exeter

To Trinity College, Cambridge

Acknowledgements

Thanks to the editors of the following magazines and anthologies, where some of these poems were first published: *Waterstone's Guide to Poetry Books, Great Gate* (Trinity College Staff Magazine), *Poetry Review, PN Review, West Bay: an Anthology* (Rocket Press), *Times Literary Supplement, The North, Weekend Guardian, Ape, London Magazine, The Seven Deadly Sins* (Brighton Festival, 1998), *The Forward Book of Poetry 1999, The Funny Side* (Faber, 1998), *The National Poetry Day Comic Verse Anthology* (Poetry Society), *The Nightwatch Girl of the Moon* (Ilkley Literature Festival, 1998), *Harvill Anthology of Twentieth-Century Poetry* (Harvill, 1999) and *Mosaic* (Penguin Books India, 1999).

Some of the poems were commissioned for Friends of the Earth/Big Wide Words *Poems on the Buses* exhibitions.

Contents

(iii)

(i)

Occupational Hazard

He has slept with accountants and brokers,
With a cowgirl (well, someone from Healds).
He has slept with non-smokers and smokers
In commercial and cultural fields.

He has slept with book-keepers, book-binders,
Slept with auditors, florists, PAs,
Child psychologists, even child minders,
With directors of firms and of plays.

He has slept with the stupid and clever.
He has slept with the rich and the poor
But he sadly admits that he's never
Slept with a poet before.

Real poets are rare, he confesses,
While it's easy to find a cashier.
So I give him some poets' addresses
And consider a change of career.

This Morning in a Black Jag

In this ringroad-and-roundabout business park of a place,
Where the favourite phrases are modem and user-base
And a poet is probably seen as a waste of space,
I'm in need of a mode of transport and a familiar face

And I seem to have picked up a car with a man that drives –
Whenever I order a cab, it is he who arrives,
Drops me off at my nines and collects me from my fives,
And although for the bulk of the days we lead totally separate lives,

When I mentioned some places up north, he knew where they were,
And he even conceded Oasis were better than Blur,
And Jim Morrison blares from his cab, though he says he'd prefer
To be thought of not as a taxi driver but as a chauffeur.

To prove it, he turned up this morning in a black Jag,
And, while teaching bored youths how to write is no less of a drag
(You're explaining the sonnet, they're planning which lessons to
    wag),
It's more bearable when you turn up in a car about which you
    can brag.

Stroppy kids can't depress me – I'm lucky enough to have found
A man who leaves every day free just to drive me around,
Who asks how it went and who tells me which schools are
    renowned
For reducing the squeamish to tears. We have covered a fair bit
    of ground

And we secretly wonder (we're both too polite to enquire)
Why his fares are much lower these days, why my tips are much
    higher,
Why our journeys get longer each time, so we tend to go via
This diversion or that, both pretending there's scenery there to
    admire.

For our last trip, he charges me half the original quote:
Just two pounds, but he gets the change from my five pound note
And I get the smell of his Jaguar on my coat
And a train journey home to read and re-read the receipts he wrote.

Your Dad Did What?

Where they have been, if they have been away,
or what they've done at home, if they have not –
you make them write about the holiday.
One writes *My Dad did*. What? Your Dad did what?

That's not a sentence. Never mind the bell.
We stay behind until the work is done.
You count their words (you who can count and spell);
all the assignments are complete bar one

and though this boy seems bright, that one is his.
He says he's finished, doesn't want to add
anything, hands it in just as it is.
No change. *My Dad did*. What? What did his Dad?

You find the 'E' you gave him as you sort
through reams of what this girl did, what that lad did,
and read the line again, just one 'e' short:
This holiday was horrible. My Dad did.

His First If Lady Only Just

I am the country of his fame;
his constitution knows I am.
With half a presidential name
he's my no-Lincoln Abraham.

Now that's a bit below the belt
he says, when relevant, to show
that while he ain't no Roosevelt
he's no mean Franklin Delano.

I throw his party left and right
and, like a Herbert chases dust,
I chase him all around the White,
his First if Lady only just.

I blow his mind but not his brains –
half-presidents are safe, I guess.
No Johnson but a Lyndon Baines,
a truer man than Harry S.

I am the country of his fame,
the Nancy who creates the Ron,
the one he's bound to shoot or frame
when all the love has pentagon.

Rondeau Redoublé

He likes the soup but doesn't like the spoon.
We hold opposing views on means and ends.
It's funny now, but it would matter soon
If we shared more than chinese food and friends.

In case he breaks the only time he bends,
He drinks the coffee, leaves the macaroon.
He says, as though pure anarchy descends,
He likes the soup but doesn't like the spoon.

I've sat in restaurants all afternoon,
Fallen for all the culinary trends
But to admit this seems inopportune.
We hold opposing views on means and ends.

Normally I am someone who defends
High living, but I let him call the tune
During these strange, occasional weekends.
It's funny now, but it would matter soon;

The earth won't sprout a ladder to the moon
Though we make compromises and amends.
It would be like December next to June
If we shared more than chinese food and friends.

Sometimes we clash, sometimes our difference blends
And the cold air turns hot in the balloon.
I tell myself (in case success depends
On attitude) that though he hates the spoon,
He likes the soup.

The Yellow and the Blue

Could be an armband or a rubber ring,
a lilo or a surfboard or a boat,
a wave (it needn't be a man-made thing)
that makes it briefly possible to float;
could be the lotion I slap on, rub in
to give the sun the temper of the shade,
or the umbrella that relieves my skin
while others turn to leather and to suede;
could be that in the pool or on the beach,
could be that in the yellow and the blue,
the tourist's miracles within my reach
are not commissioned or inspired by you,
and if to me you're block, board, ring and band
I am, as much as this is not, your land.

Against Road-building

He hated roads. He loved the land.
He tended to forget
Or else he didn't understand
That roads were how we met.

He loved long walks. He hated cars.
He often put them down.
Without them, though, I'd have reached Mars
Before I reached his town.

Now that I've seen bad air pervade
An atmosphere once sweet
I wish the car was never made
That drove me to his street.

Now that I've felt a world explode
As I had not before
I wish they'd never built the road
That led me to his door.

None of the Blood

None of the blood that is in your body
   is in my body. None of the blood
      that is in my body is in your body.
Whatever you are, you are not my blood.

None of the flesh that is on your body
   is on my body. None of the flesh
      that is on my body is on your body.
Whatever you are, you are not my flesh.

I have shared a bottle of wine with a bigot
   (none of the eggshells, none of the mud
      in my kitchen and garden, your kitchen and garden).
None of the flesh. None of the blood

that is in my kitchen is in your kitchen.
   (I am being rude. I am not just being rude.)
      None of your garden is in my garden.
I have shared a picnic bench with a prude.

Furniture, yes, means of transport, yes,
   but no to soul and no to bone
      (none of your sellotape, none of your glue).
Yes to some stranger. No to you.

Marrying the Ugly Millionaire

Here comes my mother carrying
Dried flowers for my hair.
This afternoon I'm marrying
The ugly millionaire.

Here is my sister with the veil.
Everyone wants to share
My lucrative unholy grail –
The ugly millionaire.

There are our presents, wrapped and tied.
Soon they will fill the room.
All marked (no mention of the bride)
Attention of the groom –

No Dior, no St Laurent, no frills,
No full Le Creuset set.
Only my father's unpaid bills,
My brother's gambling debt,

Demands beyond and way above
What would be right or fair.
I hate the grasping lot. I love
The ugly millionaire.

The Wise One

I could not scrub the lift shaft with a toothbrush,
Spare time to stitch new bookmarks out of lace
Or carry boxes up and down rope ladders.
I'm not the helpful one around this place.
The helpful one is over there with a chipped marble face.

I will not press a calculator's buttons,
Clock in, tot up, give coins as change from notes.
I'm not the numbers one. Haven't they told you
How dizzy I am from counting last year's votes?
The numbers one is on the slab, under a pile of coats.

Don't come to me for vases of carnations –
I'd barely know a cactus from a rose.
Consult the experts for the best arrangements,
Flowery ones. I am not one of those.
The flowery one is in the earth, with everything that grows.

I haven't seen the overhead projector
This week. I cannot just nip down the road.
I'm not the knowing one, I'm not the going one,
Or the finding one. Those three are being towed
To a farm to be written out of a crucial episode.

Which one am I? I must be one. Everyone else is.
Look at those little pet other ones, shining their knees,
No doubts as to which ones they are. Which one am I?
The answering one, the resolving one? Neither of these.
Try the wise one, the free one, but only if everyone else agrees.

Ruining the Volunteer

I'm ruining the volunteer today.
I get through sometimes nine or ten a year,
Or even more, if more are sent my way.
Today I'm ruining the volunteer.

I first suggest he asks for decent wages,
More than his measly travel reimbursed.
We're still in the preliminary stages.
It's always worth suggesting wages first.

The volunteer denies he's on the breadline
Because thus far he's had his bread with jam.
He practises liasing with a deadline
As if my sound advice weren't worth a damn.

He'll learn at his expense for his expenses.
Tomorrow, volunteer, you'll be assailed
By demonstrations of what common sense is
And words you never use, words like curtailed,

Buffeted, buttressed, bulwark, bolstered, bounded –
Powerful words with plenty to express.
Tomorrow, volunteer, you'll be surrounded
By those who wouldn't leave their beds for less.

So pick me up at six in my pyjamas,
Put on my gloves and coat, pull up my hood.
This is how postmen feel, postmen and farmers.
Oh, stop complaining. It will do you good

Or put you off. I hinder and delay you
For your own good. For mine, you leap ahead.
I'm neither able nor inclined to pay you.
Volunteer, I cannot get out of bed.

Four Sonnets

UNSAVOURY (COULD ALMOST PASS FOR SWEET)

He parks where he is not allowed to park
and does what he is ill-advised to do.
As reassuring as a question mark,
his words are neither sensible nor true
but still I let him know that he's preferred.
His nod confirms that he can be discreet.
The way he twists the meaning of a word
unsavoury could almost pass for sweet.

Sweet: in my weaker moments, everyone
rallies around and soon I have a list
of twenty reasons why I ought to run.
My reason is the only one they've missed:
not all the bad things he may do or be
but that he's better at them all than me.

NEVER HIS

I freeze as I'm about to write his name.
Politely, he reminds me who he is.
What can I say that won't sound trite or lame –
I could forget some names, but never his?
So I say nothing, simply write it down,
hand him the envelope and let him leave,
though I'm inclined to chase him all round town
to put this right, tamper with clocks, retrieve
the eyes that wavered and the hand that shook,
the hesitation he perceived as tact,
the blush he understandably mistook
for loss of memory (which now, in fact,
is sharper than it was, and will replay
him telling me his name all night, all day).

TYPECASTING

Not knowing you, I thought I knew your type –
how you'd behave, the sort of thing you'd say.
I guessed you'd be inclined to take a swipe
at anybody getting in your way.
I told my friends you were like this, like that,
had you evading taxes, cutting throats,
gave you a line in patronising chat,
presented my imaginings as quotes.
But your behaviour is exemplary.
Your words have been, without exception, kind.
Do you have preconceived ideas of me?
If I am not yet typecast in your mind,
can I suggest the fool who will insist
on putting words in mouths she should have kissed?

SOMETHING INVOLVING US

I was so drunk, I don't remember much –
not how your body felt and not your arms
around me, not your dinner-suited touch
between two cars (not setting off alarms).
I do remember, though, the next day's drink,
your calmness, your I-still-respect-you smile,
and I remember that you said, 'I think
it's better if we leave it for a while.'
I next remember that you changed your mind,
and changed your mind, and changed your mind again,
as if, for you, something remained behind
(something I missed, not being sober then)
from that first night, something involving us,
that makes what's happened since seem worth the fuss.

Diminishing Returns

I will tell outright lies where you embellish.
Your yawn will be my cue to fall asleep.
Anyone who is watching us with relish
Will find that, where your talk and tricks are cheap,
Mine will be cast-offs. When you stop at kissing
I'll stop at shaking hands; you eye the clock,
I'll grab my watch and gasp at what I'm missing
And any door you close, I'll double-lock.
Operate slowly – I'll stand still for ever.
Leave quickly – I will be the speed of light
Passing you on the way, and if we never
Do anything constructive, that's all right
(Though it will be a wasted chance) because
While casual observers say of you
'He led her on', of me they'll say, 'She was
The less enthusiastic of the two.'

This Calculating Field

A threatened field knows that it must give way
to a new road, starts to prepare for change,
turns, in anticipation, almost grey.
Everyone says *doesn't the grass look strange?*

The green that once inspired them to protest
has lost its charm, character, former fame.
Change can now safely be compared to rest.
The grass turns grey, ready to take the blame

as well as all effects of the assault.
Forget the luxury of looking good;
assume control. *Yes it is all my fault.*
If I did not turn bad, somebody would.

Can I have won and at the same time lost
all of my qualities that once appealed?
The outcome of a benefit and cost
equation is this calculating field

turning to grey. Your sadness in defending
becomes exhilaration in attack.
I can imagine only one good ending:
where you are glad that I will not be back.

Leaving and Leaving You

When I leave your postcode and your commuting station,
When I leave undone the things that we planned to do
You may feel you have been left by association
But there is leaving and there is leaving you.

When I leave your town and the club that you belong to,
When I leave without much warning or much regret
Remember, there's doing wrong and there's doing wrong to
You, which I'll never do and I haven't yet,

And when I have gone, remember that in weighing
Everything up, from love to a cheaper rent,
You were all the reasons I thought of staying
And you were none of the reasons why I went

And although I leave your sight and I leave your setting
And our separation is soon to be a fact,
Though you stand beside what I'm leaving and forgetting,
I'm not leaving you, not if motive makes the act.

(ii)

A Division Fence

Dictate to me my house   you the more clever
the more aware   our past has consequences

      the purchaser's heirs and assigns will make and forever
      hereafter maintain a division fence or fences

whisper   *restrictive covenant*   whenever
they hover in the grounds   you the more gifted

      the purchaser's heirs and assigns will make and forever

whisper   *restrictive covenant unlifted*

whisper   *so heavy with the weight of lawyers*
my fence   *in stick three names together firms*
They hover in the grounds   weak wood destroyers
whisper   *strong wood*   *strong wood*   Dictate the terms

They are a slow man's marathon from harmless
What do we like? Clean and straightforward Deeds
here at the firm of Grudge Successful Charmless

oh let me let me let me in it pleads

misunderstanding   fence *neurotic* border
Stand firm   *fence fence* the firm of Brick Flesh Wood
No heir of mine and no assign to order
oh let you in   as if your Deeds were good

Next Door Despised

Next door despised
your city. They would much prefer a town.
Your tree – they'd like a twig.
Your oil rig,
your salmon satin crown,
so can you cut it down and cut it down?

Next door began
a harsh campaign. They hired a ticket tout
to sell your oily tree,
your haddocky
crown for a well of drought,
and then they bricked it up and shut it out.

Next door perceived
an envelope was lying on your stoop
but no one wrote to them
so your silk hem
deserved their mushroom soup.
Next door made plans to follow you to group

therapy, pinch
your problems, change their characters and looks.
Next door alleged your streams
gave them bad dreams.
Couldn't you call them brooks?
Couldn't you write some better, shorter books?

Next door observed
your shoulder stump, asked what was up your sleeve,
swore that they meant no harm,
said that to arm
dictators was naïve
(no pun intended). Next door don't believe

you've gone to work,
neither the place nor the activity.
While next door's squirrel slipped,
your manuscript
lolled on the balcony
which might seem natural to you or me

but to next door
it was a gate wide enough to admit
the dwarves in overcoats
who chase weak votes,
whose coffee smells of shit,
whose stubble shakes only when candle-lit.

Next door have got
their own house but they choose to squat in yours.
If you brought up their theft
of what was left
and asked whose ceilings, floors
and walls these were, next door would say next door's.

Barbecue!

I can afford to lose a window pane,
for once a month a brandy glass to break.
He is related to the hurricane.
I tolerate its visits for his sake.

Tracing his tree directly to the flood
we float a lot, but as he pointed out
we remain dry beside the running mud
courtesy of his ancestor the drought.

Our food is either ash or somehow scarred.
Barbecue! he announces, for the fire
is his relation too, one of the charred
tastes (or disasters) I must now acquire.

All this would matter if we'd met by chance
but I, for all his kinship to the quake,
spring from the siren and the ambulance.
One rumble and my foot comes off the brake.

Like Carnivals

I thought I saw you pass in the parade,
masked on a float or clapping in the crowd,
and was persuaded by the sense it made
that among many, one might be allowed

(one random body at the hotdog stand
or chance extension of the burger queue,
trombone or trumpet player in the band,
even a clown) to turn out to be you.

At all events where people congregate
like carnivals and festivals and balls
I seek our little world within the great,
turning horizons into bedroom walls.

The Burning Scheme

The newly burned are queuing in the shop,
leaf-fall-in-autumn jigsaws on their skin.
Everyone only wants the pain to stop
      as they survey the crop
of Delial, Ambre Solaire, Piz Buin.
There is no lotion for the burn within.

The newly dazed are tethered to a wink.
Left eyes stand guard while right eyes squint and seep.
Everything has been tried: pills, a hot drink,
      a cream containing zinc,
everything that is popular and cheap.
The burn within thrives on a good night's sleep.

Moon like an orange in a sea of gin,
apply your coolness to a burning dream.
Hat with a mess thereunder, lift your chin,
      lift all the teeth therein.
How do you fit into the burning scheme,
hat of the famous England cricket team?

The burn within makes no attempt to cheat.
Its pockets, so to speak, are free of sand.
Fairly it wins and squarely it can beat
      every burn caused by heat,
hops on a night flight home, keen to expand
in the wet climate of its native land.

She Has Established Title

She keeps the lies and popular support.
I take the condemnation and the truth.
I claim the chase; she has already caught.
Her permanence is balanced by my youth.
The afternoons are mine. She hogs the nights,
The public sphere encompassed by her rings.
She has established title. All the rights
Are hers. How fairly we divide these things.
Each of us has a quite substantial list
Of goodies, and I wouldn't choose to swap,
Like football cards, the knowledge I exist
For both the mortgage and the weekly shop,
My inventory for hers, if someone were
To ask, or wonder, what I might prefer.

The Bridging Line

If, as it now appears,
a second time can lean across the ditch,
retrieve, like a dropped stitch,
the first, long in arrears,
how badly I've misjudged the last five years;

potholes beside our past
I thought they were, when all the time they've been
linear, in between,
travelling (if not fast)
towards next time, back from next time to last.

Tonight's no precipice,
merely one station on the bridging line
where incidents combine,
kiss throws a rope to kiss,
last time connects to next, next time to this –

a better fairytale
than scattered breadcrumbs on the forest floor;
wind howls, rain starts to pour
and soon you've lost your trail.
The bridging line is like a polished rail

beneath our years of space
that I can almost rest my hand upon.
I clutch it now you're gone,
find it reflects your face,
find I believe the next five years will race

straightforwardly ahead
as five have raced straightforwardly behind.
The gaps are redefined.
I hold my breath and tread
the bridging line towards a waiting bed.

Your Darlings

You call some women Darling and they fall
predictably in love, but say the same
to others (brighter ones, perhaps) and all
it means, they say, is that you're scared you'll call
one woman by another woman's name.

I know you get around a bit (I ought
to know) but can't presume to guess your fears
or what proportion of your conquests thought
your Darlings were sincere, or if the sort
of woman who believes her hopes and ears

predominates over the doubting kind
in your portfolio, whether a lapse
in disbelief makes a believing mind,
the lucky owner waking up to find
her prospects changed (to brighter ones, perhaps).

Some hunt and hunt until they find a fake
behind what either was or sounded true.
Those who are anything like me will take
the best interpretation, maybe make
fools of themselves, but make the most of you.

His Bounceability on Knees

She wound the scarf tightly around her eyes
thinking that if she couldn't see at all
she might forget that such a thing as size
existed, and pretend he wasn't small
but all the scarf blocked out was half the light;
his stunted shape persisted through the gauze
and she still knew that he was half her height
despite their flat shoes and the level floors
and all that she had seen in him at first,
things like his bounceability on knees,
did nothing but contribute to her thirst
for what was out of reach, past clouds and trees,
when – far above the skull that she could feel
against her thigh – racing around her head
were visions of a large, departing heel
shaking the nearby woodland with its tread.

Over and Elm and I

Nothing to recommend your feet
except that when you put them down
on Market Hill or Benet Street
you make a better town

Nothing to recommend your stance
except that anywhere you stand
soaks up your presence to enhance
all the surrounding land

No evidence you are a cure
but that the envelope you sealed
and hand-delivered to my door
held a St Neots field

Nothing but that you seem to reach
beyond the space you occupy
so that in March and Waterbeach
Over and Elm and Eye

pillows store imprints of your face
surprised to learn that there's a head
whose contact with a pillowcase
can so improve a bed

You hailed a taxi at the lights
now every single cab that turns
onto East Road like yours ignites
Even the downpour burns

In its stone pot the stand-up clock
turns to a flower on its stem
The county's little stations rock
I feel like one of them

Once When the Wind Blew

Our purses and our fumes
distinguish us, the normals, drys and oilies
who scan the tablecloths in auction rooms,
churn up the paper doilies

to find a cleaner head,
phrenology's bald, ornamental scalps,
black virtues sprinkled and black vices spread
on curves as white as Alps.

If we abandoned hair,
if, in its place, we could contrive to grow
lists of our qualities, complete but fair,
best and worst points on show,

the pain that it would save,
the moves from double into separate beds.
Imagine they are coming to engrave,
tomorrow, all our heads

and now's the time to dump
all that we judge unfit for public view.
We're talking ink (an enigmatic bump
is always subject to

interpretation, doubt,
with how it feels depending on the hand).
I would far rather have it all spelled out,
easy to understand.

Would I have felt that twinge
of sadness if I'd seen the word *inert*,
once when the wind blew, underneath your fringe,
or been so badly hurt

if just above your ear
capacity to cause unhappiness . . .
I could extend this game and this idea
but heads do not confess

failings to clumps of hair,
nor leave them stranded when the hair is gone,
but I know yours and when we meet somewhere
I'm going to carve them on.

Hardly Dear

I wouldn't buy you from a car boot sale,
not if your mind had been reduced to clear,
though you were overpriced at half a year.
With your significance cut down to scale

I could afford you. If you soon turned stale
I could point out that you were hardly dear
and that I'd had my money's worth, or near.
I wouldn't buy you from a car boot sale,

you or a size five shoe or books in braille –
I have no use for them. Let the sincere
stall-holder smile and say *a snip, a mere*
pittance as though he flogged the holy grail,

the greatest bargain in this hemisphere
rather than just a load of useless gear.
He might succeed with some. With me he'd fail.
I wouldn't buy you from a car boot sale.

Nobody Said You Had to Come

Why did you come to this workshop if you didn't want to write?
I can think of at least ten other things you could have done tonight.
As for good soaps you could have watched, there were an easy three.
Nobody said you had to come and spend two hours with me.

You're happy to drink a cup of tea and eat a chocolate biscuit
But asked to write some poetry, you'd prefer not to risk it
So are you here by accident? Was it an oversight?
Why did you come to this workshop if you didn't want to write?

You tell me firmly several times, to check I've understood,
That nothing I can say or do could make your poems good.
I am an optimist but I agree the chance is slight,
So why did you come to this workshop if you didn't want to write?

Did a vindictive spouse propel you here against your will
When all you wanted was to stay at home and watch *The Bill*?
Why, when I mention poems, do your eyes pop out in fright
And why did you come to this workshop if you didn't want to write?

The sign says *Writing Poetry*, which, I feel, makes it plain
That poetry will be involved, will even be the main
Activity on offer. It's spelled out in black and white.
Why did you come to this workshop if you didn't want to write?

Let me point out I'm doing this for money not for fun.
I don't care if you write or not. You're not the only one
Who will greet nine o'clock with unequivocal delight
But why did you come to the workshop if you didn't want to write?

Most of you spell quite well, so it's unlikely you've misread
Poetry and concluded it was *Pottery* instead.
Would you become a pilot, then refuse to board the flight?
Why did you come to this workshop if you didn't want to write?

All right then, if I'm under a complete misapprehension
And if producing poetry was never your intention,
Write a short piece of prose explaining why you're here, in spite
Of having not a lot to say and no desire to write.

If People Disapprove of You . . .

Make being disapproved of your hobby.
Make being disapproved of your aim.
Devise new ways of scoring points
In the Being Disapproved Of Game.

Let them disapprove in their dozens.
Let them disapprove in their hoards.
You'll find that being disapproved of
Builds character, brings rewards

Just like any form of striving.
Don't be arrogant; don't coast
On your high disapproval rating.
Try to be disapproved of most.

At this point, if it's useful,
Draw a pie chart or a graph.
Show it to someone who disapproves.
When they disapprove, just laugh.

Count the emotions you provoke:
Anger, suspicion, shock.
One point for each of these and two
For every boat you rock.

Feel yourself warming to your task –
You do it bloody well.
At last you've found an area
In which you can excel.

Savour the thrill of risk without
The fear of getting caught.
Whether they sulk or scream or pout,
Enjoy your new-found sport.

Meanwhile, all those who disapprove
While you are having fun
Won't even know your game exists
So tell yourself you've won.

(iii)

Tribute

For the first time I find it quite unnerving
That people's names are handed on to things.
No bench, so far, has proved itself deserving
Enough to bear your name. No hospice wings
Or students' union buildings will inherit,
If it has anything to do with me,
A name no other man could even merit
Let alone any slice of brick or tree.
I could be Lord Mayor with a town to listen
To my new street names; you would still be gone.
Now, as myself, with power to rechristen
No roads, there's still a tribute going on:
Though I call nothing by your name, I do
Practically nothing but call after you.

The blister on my heel has healed.
Each day there's more between
This laundry and the lake and field,
What is and what has been,
Or, by the currents of our blood,
Me and a future queen.

Each day, each minute, hauls the mud
From the concealing mist
And strips the glamour from the dud,
Gauze from the fractured wrist
But I have soared too high in rank
For us to co-exist.

I thank all those I ought to thank
But I am in the place
Of every miracle that sank
With or without a trace.
As if all smiles were mine by right
I robbed a mouthless face.

Each seventh generation night
Revives the ankle sprain,
The sound of static and the slight
Psychosis of the rain.
The moss that issues from her slab
Furs my approaching train.

The blister on my heel's a scab.
I am no longer dressed
In swamp, or bleeding in a cab
Bound for a shrine South West
But lots of things were crushed and lost
When we became the best.

I am supporting S
as if I were a bean
under his c
though he is not a
Under his c
a nightmare is a di

Steven and I have
Some people have
I would be t
to cheer for Steven
I would be t
to fail if Steven trie

I am supporting Ste
as if I were a rail
behind his cu
though he is bound
Behind his cu
a white net is a veil.

Steven is no perform
He has no gift for sp
I make no coo
by staging my supp
I make no coo
adorn no tennis cour

but I am supporting
as if I were a pin
above his hem
though he will never
Above his hem
a jacket is a skin.

Tribute

For the first time I find it quite unnerving
That people's names are handed on to things.
No bench, so far, has proved itself deserving
Enough to bear your name. No hospice wings
Or students' union buildings will inherit,
If it has anything to do with me,
A name no other man could even merit
Let alone any slice of brick or tree.
I could be Lord Mayor with a town to listen
To my new street names; you would still be gone.
Now, as myself, with power to rechristen
No roads, there's still a tribute going on:
Though I call nothing by your name, I do
Practically nothing but call after you.

The League of Saints

The blister on my heel has healed.
Each day there's more between
This laundry and the lake and field,
What is and what has been,
Or, by the currents of our blood,
Me and a future queen.

Each day, each minute, hauls the mud
From the concealing mist
And strips the glamour from the dud,
Gauze from the fractured wrist
But I have soared too high in rank
For us to co-exist.

I thank all those I ought to thank
But I am in the place
Of every miracle that sank
With or without a trace.
As if all smiles were mine by right
I robbed a mouthless face.

Each seventh generation night
Revives the ankle sprain,
The sound of static and the slight
Psychosis of the rain.
The moss that issues from her slab
Furs my approaching train.

The blister on my heel's a scab.
I am no longer dressed
In swamp, or bleeding in a cab
Bound for a shrine South West
But lots of things were crushed and lost
When we became the best.

I could have easily been tossed,
Demented, in the lake,
As popular as an embossed
Horse mistress at the wake.
She and I share the strength to hoist
Our men above the rake

And I, and no doubt she, rejoiced
When it at last transpired
That all the prayers we'd rasped and voiced
And all the bombs we'd wired
Blew us towards the league of saints
We worshipped and admired.

The visors, boiler-suits and paints
All add to the effect.
Likewise if someone shrieks or faints,
Likewise if lives are wrecked
And silent in the music booth
The founder of our sect,

His schizophrenic glaze of youth.
Processional, we stalk.
Whether I'm closer to his truth
Than islands in New York,
The blister on my heel has healed.
Take up your shoe and walk.

Steven's Side

I am supporting Steven
as if I were a beam
        under his ceiling, even
though he is not a team.
        Under his ceiling even
a nightmare is a dream.

Steven and I have entered.
Some people have implied
        I would be too self-centred
to cheer for Steven's side,
        I would be too self-centred
to fail if Steven tried.

I am supporting Steven
as if I were a rail
        behind his curtain, even
though he is bound to fail.
        Behind his curtain even
a white net is a veil.

Steven is no performer.
He has no gift for sport.
        I make no cool crowd warmer
by staging my support.
        I make no cool crowd warmer,
adorn no tennis court

but I am supporting Steven
as if I were a pin
        above his hemline, even
though he will never win.
        Above his hemline even
a jacket is a skin.

I am supporting Steven.
I am at Steven's feet.
    I put him first and even
give him a thing to beat.
    I put him first and even
then he will not compete.

In Wokingham on Boxing Day
at The Edinburgh Woollen Mill

Two earnest customers compare
a ribbed and unribbed sleeve.
I wonder what I'm doing here
and think I ought to leave,
get in my car and drive away.
       I stand beside the till
       in Wokingham on Boxing Day
       at The Edinburgh Woollen Mill.

All of the other shops are closed.
Most people are in bed.
Somehow I know that I'm supposed
to find an A-Z.
Somehow I sense I must obey
       an unfamiliar will
       in Wokingham on Boxing Day
       at The Edinburgh Woollen Mill.

I parked in a disabled space
so either I'm a cheat
or a debilitating case
of searching for your street
has started to erode away
       my locomotive skill
       in Wokingham on Boxing Day
       at The Edinburgh Woollen Mill,

somewhere perhaps you've never been.
I doubt you're into wool.
Even if mohair's not your scene
the atmosphere is full
of your proximity. I sway
       and feel a little ill
       in Wokingham on Boxing Day
       at The Edinburgh Woollen Mill.

The sales assistants wish me luck
and say they hope I find
the place I want. I have been stuck
with what I left behind,
with what I've been too scared to say,
        too scared to say until
        in Wokingham on Boxing Day
        at The Edinburgh Woollen Mill

I tell myself the time is now;
willingly I confess
my love for you to some poor cow
in an angora dress
whose *get lost loony* eyes convey
        her interest, which is nil,
        in Wokingham on Boxing Day
        at The Edinburgh Woollen Mill.

I find your house. You're still in bed.
I leave my gift and flee,
pleased with myself, not having said
how you can contact me,
driven by fears I can't allay,
        dreams I did not fulfil
        in Wokingham on Boxing Day
        at The Edinburgh Woollen Mill.

Chains are the most distressing shops.
They crop up everywhere.
The point at which the likeness stops
squeezes my lungs of air.
When I see jumpers on display
        I wish that I was still
        in Wokingham on Boxing Day
        at The Edinburgh Woollen Mill.

Three Light Sign

There is a certain railway line
that runs straight through your town.
The level crossing's three light sign,
a therefore upside down,

has never blocked my route to you.
Perhaps my speed alarms
its sense of pace. When I drive through
the crossing's up in arms

but it has never told me stop
so I have never learned.
Attempts at sense have been a flop,
a therefore overturned.

You're always either in your room
or wandering about
outside. The crossing, I assume,
knows not to let you out.

I like to think it's in control
in case I go too far.
How underrated, on the whole,
most level crossings are.

You've given me a few bad nights –
ranting, withdrawn or worse
but when I see the crossing lights,
a therefore in reverse,

I know you don't mean any harm.
That's just the way it goes.
You, like the level crossing arm,
must have your highs and lows.

Sometimes two things that shouldn't mix
cannot be kept apart.
There is a rift too deep to fix
between a stop, a start,

a car, a train. But I see ways
over contested land,
watching the level crossing raise
its firm, permissive hand.

Driving Me Away

I caught the train to Waterloo,
The tube to Leicester Square.
Both did what they set out to do,
But neither could compare
With your closed eyes, your bitten nails
And the oddness you display.
You beat whatever's on the rails
At driving me away.

The coach to Gatwick last July
Did it in record time.
The plane, once it had deigned to fly,
Managed an upward climb.
You beat whatever's in the air
Or on the motorway
And do not even charge a fare
For driving me away.

The transit van I hired to move
For which I had to pack
Box after box, as if to prove
I wasn't coming back
And before driving which I paid
A visit to the tip,
Just to ensure the point was made:
This was a one way trip –

You beat that too. I could name loads
Of engine-powered things
In oceans, in the clouds, on roads,
With carriages or wings
But you could nudge them all off track
With the mad things you say.
No car could ever have your knack
Of driving me away.

There's not a lot that you can do
Well, or indeed at all.
I must appreciate your few
Talents. When taxis stall
Or when friends offer me a lift
And there's a slight delay
I am reminded of your gift
For driving me away.

Paint a Closed Window

We stood side by side.
Only George walked on.
You spoke and I replied
    but I had gone.

My gone did not depend
on anything you'd planned
and I did not extend
    even a hand.

My gone was not the sort
that might come back one day.
It was less felt than thought
    but most away.

I looked the same to you,
the arches and the cars,
and you could not see through
    my skin to bars.

My arrow pointed north.
Your word had lost its pass,
so no more back and forth
    from the hourglass.

My face became a chart
where pleasantries were drawn.
The binman pulled his cart
    around the lawn

where we stood once removed,
where we stand twice returned.
Nothing can be improved
    my gone has learned.

Foolish to have supposed
there might be other ways.
Paint a closed window, closed
     is how it stays.

I am prepared to face
how fleeting I have been
to you and to this place,
     that tree, the green

circle of grass, the stone.
From your first fixed-term kiss
I knew I could not own
     any of this.

Minus Fingers

What craftsmen sometimes do to glass
Or children to balloons,
You do (or did, since presents pass –
Shade of infrequent moons),

What lovers, as the distance grows,
Do with a hand and kiss.
Some do to bubbles or a nose
What you have done to this.

What stylists, after wash and cut,
Do to their clients' hair.
What the wind does to make doors shut
Using no more than air.

How brass band players get the sound
Out of their golden horns,
How breezes move one leaf around
Several connecting lawns,

Is how you've treated what you had,
Like football referees
To whistles when a move is bad
Enough for penalties.

You've done what someone does who spends
Money they can't afford.
So let's compare you with said friends
And see how well you've scored.

Your nose is still a chain of blocks.
Your power on the pitch
Is non-existent, Liquid-locks-
For-hair. You weren't once rich

So you enjoyed no spending spree.
You have no crystal zoo.
You can scare no one noisily
Piercing the things you blew.

You've got no notes to make a tune,
No fragile fluid spheres
To demonstrate how fast, how soon
Everything disappears,

No kiss that soars above flat land.
I count what can be shown,
In minus fingers on my hand,
For everything you've blown.

Never Away from You

*(This poem was commissioned by Friends of the Earth/
Poems on the Buses 1998, to go on a London bus.)*

Start at King's Cross and head for Waterloo.
People should read this verse from East to West,
Always towards, never away from you.

I need some kind bus drivers, just a few
To take my lines the way that I suggest:
Start at King's Cross and head for Waterloo.

Passengers at the bus stop in a queue
Must change their routes and see that mine's the best:
Always towards, never away from you.

Alternative directions will not do.
All other destinations fail my test.
Start at King's Cross and head for Waterloo.

If London Transport bosses only knew
What was at stake, they'd see my words progressed
Always towards, never away from you.

They'd help this poem get from CB2
To RG40, properly addressed,
Start at King's Cross and head for Waterloo,
Always towards, never away from you.

Men to Burn

The same man every year;
though we have men to burn
we have sealed off that idea.
It is still one man's turn.

Every year one man glows,
his bright flesh chars to dim
and every next year shows
we are not rid of him.

He is propped against a fence.
His embroidered teeth still flash.
I part with twenty pence
to convert him into ash

but he won't stay ash for long.
He reappears in rags,
features not quite so strong
and his legs in dustbin bags.

He will keep coming back
for as long as he is allowed.
He will turn from gold to black
if he knows he's got a crowd.

I should have said this before
but I'm not prepared to pay
to bring him back once more
or to make him go away.

I don't like his grey sock face
or this year's cushion knees.
A good man in the first place
makes for better effigies.

The Norbert Dentressangle Van

I heave my morning like a sack
of signs that don't appear,
say August, August, takes me back . . .
        That it was not this year . . .
say greenness, greenness, that's the link . . .
        That they were different trees
does not occur to those who think
in anniversaries.

I drive my morning like a truck
with a backsliding load,
say bastard, bastard, always stuck
        behind him on the road
(although I saw another man
        in a distinct machine
last time a Dentressangle van
was on the A14).

I draw my evening like a blind,
say darkness, darkness, that's
if not the very then the kind . . .
        That I see only slats . . .
say moonlight, moonlight, shines the same . . .
        That it's a streetlamp's glow
might be enough to take the name
from everything we know.

I sketch my evening like a plan.
I think I recognise
the Norbert Dentressangle van . . .
        That mine are clouded eyes . . .
say whiteness, whiteness, that's the shade . . .
        That paint is tins apart
might mean some progress can be made
in worlds outside the heart.